Our Favorite

Pasta

Recipes

Copyright 2006, Gooseberry Patch
First Printing, October, 2006

All rights reserved. No part of this book may be reproduced or utilized in any form or
by any means, electronic or mechanical, including photocopying and recording, or by any
information storage and retrieval system, without permission in writing from the publisher.
Printed in Korea.

Pasta Cooking Tips & Tricks

Serving pasta tonight? Put on a big pot of water to boil as soon as you get home...it'll be bubbling in no time at all!

To cook up perfect pasta, use 5 quarts of water for each pound of pasta. Bring to a rolling boil; add a tablespoon of salt, if desired. Stir in pasta; return to a rolling boil. Boil, uncovered, for the time recommended on package, stirring occasionally. Drain in a colander and toss with sauce or a little olive oil or butter.

Here's a quick & easy way to give pasta lots more flavor...just add a bouillon cube or 2 to the boiling water along with the pasta.

For chilled salads, give the cooked pasta a quick rinse in cool water and drain well...no more mushy macaroni!

For baked casseroles, cook pasta for the shortest cooking time recommended on the package. It's not necessary to rinse the cooked pasta, just drain well.

How much pasta to cook? As a general rule, pasta doubles in size when cooked, but this varies by shape. A one-pound package will serve about 4 to 8 people, depending on portion size and other ingredients.

Save extra cooked pasta for another meal…easy! Toss with a little olive oil to coat pasta, cover tightly and keep refrigerated for 3 to 4 days. To reheat, just place in a metal colander and immerse in a pot of boiling water for one minute, then drain…ready to serve!

Create a cozy Italian restaurant feel for your next pasta dinner. Toss a red & white checked tablecloth over the table, light drip candles in empty bottles and add a basket of garlic bread.

4

Creamy Chicken Spaghetti

Makes 8 servings

2 lbs. boneless, skinless
    chicken breasts, cooked
    and shredded
2 14-1/2 oz. cans stewed
    tomatoes, chopped
2 10-3/4 oz. cans cream of
    chicken soup

10-3/4 oz. can cream of
    mushroom soup
4-oz. can sliced mushrooms,
    drained
8-oz. pkg. pasteurized process
    cheese spread, cubed
16-oz. pkg. spaghetti, cooked

Combine all ingredients in a large saucepan; mix well. Cook over
medium heat until warmed through and cheese is melted.

Look for old restaurant serving dishes at
flea markets and antique shops...they're roomy enough
to hold the largest family recipes.

Salsa Ranch Skillet

Makes 4 to 6 servings

1 lb. ground beef
1/2 c. sweet onion, chopped
1/2 c. green pepper, chopped
2.8-oz. pkg. ranch salad
    dressing mix
15-oz. can tomato sauce

1 c. water
16-oz. jar mild salsa
16-oz. can baked beans
8-oz. pkg. rotini, uncooked
1 c. shredded Colby & Monterey
    Jack cheese

Brown ground beef, onion and pepper in a skillet over medium heat; drain. Stir in dressing mix until well blended. Add tomato sauce, water, salsa and beans; bring to a boil. Stir in uncooked rotini; reduce to medium-low heat and simmer for 12 to 15 minutes until tender, stirring occasionally. Remove from heat. Sprinkle with cheese and let stand for 5 minutes, until cheese melts and sauce thickens.

Let your kids plan the family dinner once a week. Younger children can practice basic cooking skills, while older kids and teens might enjoy choosing and preparing ethnic or specialty meals.

Sausage Fettuccine

Makes 4 servings

1 lb. ground Italian pork
    sausage
1 onion, chopped
1 to 2 cloves garlic, chopped
2 T. all-purpose flour

1 pt. half-and-half
2 to 3 T. grated Parmesan
    cheese
salt and pepper to taste
8-oz. pkg. fettuccine, cooked

Brown sausage, onion and garlic in a skillet over medium heat;
drain. Whisk in remaining ingredients except fettuccine; heat through
without boiling. Spoon over cooked fettuccine.

Watch for old-fashioned clear glass canisters
at tag sales and flea markets...perfect countertop storage
for pasta and dried beans.

10

Linguine with Garlic Sauce

Makes 4 servings

6 T. butter
16-oz. pkg. sliced mushrooms
6 cloves garlic, minced
1 t. dried rosemary
1/2 t. pepper
1/2-pt. container whipping
    cream

8-oz. pkg. linguine, cooked
8-oz. pkg. shredded mozzarella
    cheese
salt to taste
Garnish: chopped fresh parsley

Melt butter in a skillet over medium heat; add mushrooms, garlic and seasonings. Sauté for 5 minutes, until mushrooms release their juices, stirring occasionally. Stir in cream; simmer until thickened slightly, about 3 minutes. Add linguine, cheese and salt to taste; stir until cheese melts. Sprinkle with parsley.

Herb butter is scrumptious on warm bread! Blend together
softened butter and chopped fresh herbs like chives or
marjoram. Add a touch of lemon juice if you like.
Roll up in wax paper and chill, then slice to serve.

Chicken Cacciatore

Makes 2 to 4 servings

1 lb. boneless, skinless
   chicken breasts, cubed
2 T. oil
28-oz. jar spaghetti sauce
14-1/2 oz. can diced tomatoes

1 green pepper, diced
1 onion, diced
2 cloves garlic, minced
1 t. Italian seasoning
8-oz. pkg. spaghetti, cooked

Sauté chicken in oil over medium heat until golden; drain. Stir in remaining ingredients except spaghetti; simmer over low heat until vegetables are tender. Serve over cooked spaghetti.

The easiest-ever way to cook egg noodles...bring water to a
rolling boil, then turn off heat. Add noodles and let stand
for 20 minutes, stirring twice. Perfect!

Better-Than-Ever Beef Stroganoff *Makes 4 servings*

1-1/2 lbs. beef round steak,
    sliced into thin strips
1/4 c. all-purpose flour
pepper to taste
1/2 c. butter
4-oz. can sliced mushrooms,
    drained
1/2 c. onion, chopped

1 clove garlic, minced
10-1/2 oz. can beef broth
10-3/4 oz. can cream of
    mushroom soup
8-oz. container sour cream
8-oz. pkg. medium egg noodles,
    cooked

Toss beef strips with flour and pepper to coat. In a large skillet over medium heat, brown beef in butter. Add mushrooms, onion and garlic; sauté until tender. Stir in broth; reduce heat to low, cover and simmer for one hour. Blend in soup and sour cream; heat through over low heat for about 5 minutes, without boiling. Spoon over cooked noodles to serve.

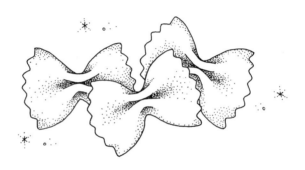

Shake up family favorite noodle dishes by using different styles
of pasta. Add interest with curly corkscrews, cavatelli shells or
wagon wheels...even spinach-flavored or rainbow pasta.

Italian Bean & Sausage Pasta   *Makes 4 servings*

6-oz. pkg. smoked turkey
    sausage, halved lengthwise
    and sliced
14-1/2 oz. can Italian-style
    stewed tomatoes
14-1/2 oz. can Italian-style
    green beans, drained
2 c. cooked rotini
1/4 c. grated Parmesan cheese

Brown sausage in a skillet over medium heat; drain. Add tomatoes
and beans; bring to a boil for 2 to 3 minutes. Stir in cooked rotini and
heat through; sprinkle with Parmesan cheese.

Serve pasta in a warmed serving bowl...a nice touch.
Simply set a colander over the bowl in the sink. Drain pasta
and let stand for a minute, then toss out the water
in the bowl and fill with hot pasta and sauce.

Herbed Zucchini & Bowties

Makes 4 servings

2 T. butter
6 T. oil, divided
1 onion, chopped
1 clove garlic, chopped
1 green pepper, diced
3 zucchini, halved lengthwise
    and sliced

1 t. dried parsley
1 t. dried rosemary
1 t. dried basil
16-oz. pkg. bowties, cooked
1/2 c. grated Parmesan cheese

In a skillet over medium heat, melt butter with 2 tablespoons oil.
Add onion and garlic; sauté for 5 minutes. Stir in green pepper;
sauté for an additional 3 minutes. Stir in zucchini and herbs;
cover and cook over low heat for 5 to 8 minutes, until zucchini
is tender. Add remaining oil; toss with bowties. Sprinkle with
Parmesan cheese.

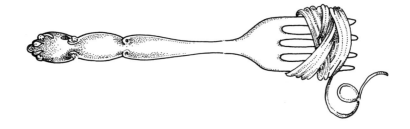

Replace spaghetti sauce in favorite pasta dishes
with mild salsa for a whole new taste.

Spaghetti with Peas & Ham

Makes 6 to 8 servings

1/4 c. butter
1 T. all-purpose flour
1/4 t. salt
1/4 t. pepper
1-1/2 c. milk
1 c. shredded mozzarella cheese

10-oz. pkg. frozen peas,
  cooked and drained
1/4 lb. sliced deli ham, cut
  into 1/8-inch strips
8-oz. pkg. spaghetti, cooked

Melt butter in a saucepan over low heat; stir in flour, salt and pepper. Add milk; cook and stir until slightly thickened. Stir in mozzarella cheese and peas; cook and stir until cheese is melted. Stir in ham; heat through. Toss with cooked spaghetti.

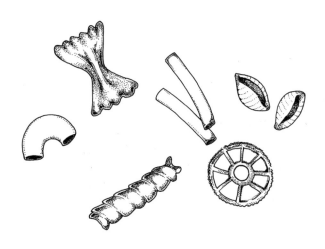

Life is a combination of magic and pasta.

-Federico Fellini

Turkey & Broccoli Alfredo

Makes 4 servings

6-oz. pkg. fettuccine, uncooked
2 c. frozen chopped broccoli
3 c. cooked turkey, cubed
10-3/4 oz. can cream of
    mushroom soup

1/2 c. milk
3/4 c. grated Parmesan cheese
1/8 t. pepper

Prepare fettuccine according to package directions, adding broccoli
in last 5 minutes of cooking; drain. Transfer mixture to a large skillet
over medium-high heat; add remaining ingredients. Cook until heated
through, stirring often.

Drizzle homemade basil pesto over warm pasta for
fresh-from-the-garden taste! Just blend 2 cups fresh basil,
2 cloves garlic, 1/2 cup grated Parmesan cheese
and 1/2 cup olive oil in the food processor...delicious!

One-Pot Spaghetti

Makes 4 servings

1 lb. ground beef
1 onion, diced
2 14-oz. cans chicken broth
6-oz. can tomato paste
1/2 t. dried oregano
1/2 t. salt

1/4 t. pepper
1/8 t. garlic powder
8-oz. pkg. spaghetti, uncooked
Garnish: grated Parmesan
    cheese

Brown ground beef and onion in a skillet over medium heat; drain and return to skillet. Stir in broth, tomato paste and seasonings; bring to a boil. Break uncooked spaghetti into short lengths and add to skillet. Reduce heat and simmer, stirring often, until spaghetti is tender, about 10 to 15 minutes. Sprinkle with Parmesan cheese.

Fresh mozzarella is delicious on baked pasta dishes
but can be difficult to grate. Freeze it first! Wrap a block
of mozzarella in plastic wrap and freeze for 20 minutes,
then grate. Store the grated cheese in a resealable
plastic zipping bag in the refrigerator for up to 5 days.

Artichoke Fettuccine

Makes 6 to 8 servings

6 T. butter
1 pt. whipping cream
8-oz. can artichokes, drained
    and chopped
1/8 t. nutmeg

1/4 c. grated Parmesan cheese
1/4 c. grated Romano cheese
1 egg yolk, beaten
16-oz. pkg. fettuccine, cooked

Melt butter in a medium saucepan over medium heat. Add cream, artichokes, nutmeg and cheeses. Stir constantly over medium heat until cheeses melt. Reduce heat to low; stir in egg yolk and continue cooking for another 3 to 5 minutes. Place fettuccine in a serving bowl; add cream mixture. Stir well and serve immediately.

Twist stems of fresh rosemary around fine wire
to form napkin rings...pleasing to the senses
with its bright green color and spicy scent.

Bacon Florentine Fettuccine

Makes 4 servings

16-oz. pkg. fettuccine,
　　uncooked
2　10-oz. pkgs. frozen creamed
　　spinach
1/2 lb. bacon, crisply cooked
　　and crumbled

1/8 t. garlic powder
1/2 c. plus 2 T. grated Parmesan
　　cheese, divided
pepper to taste

Prepare fettuccine as directed on package; drain, reserving 3/4 cup of cooking liquid. Return fettuccine and reserved liquid to saucepan. Microwave spinach as directed on package. Add spinach, bacon and garlic powder to saucepan; mix well. Transfer to a serving dish; stir in 1/2 cup Parmesan cheese. Add pepper to taste; sprinkle with remaining cheese.

Kids will love pasta dishes spooned into custard cups.
Easy to serve and just their size!

Fettuccine Alfredo

Makes 4 to 6 servings

1/2 c. butter
1 c. grated Parmesan cheese
1 pt. whipping cream

garlic salt to taste
fresh parsley to taste, chopped
16-oz. pkg. fettuccine, cooked

Melt butter in a skillet over medium-low heat. Add Parmesan cheese and mix well; stir in cream until thickened. Sprinkle with garlic salt and parsley to taste; pour over cooked fettuccine.

When cooking pasta for dinner, toss in a few eggs to hard-boil while the pasta is boiling. Then, while dinner's cooking, whip up some tasty egg salad for tomorrow's lunch!

Chicken-Broccoli Pasta

Makes 6 servings

2 4.8-oz. pkgs. herb & butter
    angel hair pasta, uncooked
1 lb. boneless, skinless chicken
    breasts, cubed

1 T. oil
10-oz. pkg. frozen chopped
    broccoli, thawed

Prepare pasta according to package directions. Sauté chicken in oil
over medium heat until golden; reduce heat and cook another
10 minutes, until juices run clear. Stir chicken and broccoli into
pasta; cook over low heat for 10 minutes, until heated through.

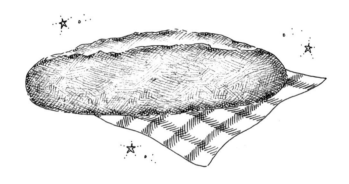

Serve an Italian feast in no time! Pesto makes a hearty appetizer when spread on crusty bread, top cooked linguine with ready-made Alfredo sauce and whip up a crispy green salad.

E-Z Beefy Macaroni

Makes 4 to 6 servings

1 lb. ground beef
28-oz. jar spaghetti sauce
8-oz. pkg. elbow macaroni,
    uncooked

8-oz. container sour cream

Brown ground beef in a skillet over medium heat; drain. Add sauce to skillet; spread uncooked macaroni in a single layer over sauce. Cover; cook over medium heat for 10 minutes, or until macaroni is tender, adding water as necessary to prevent sticking. Stir in sour cream and heat through.

Cook and chill noodles for filled pasta dishes. It'll be so much easier to fill shells and recipes will have one less step.

Basil-Asparagus Penne

Makes 4 to 6 servings

2 T. olive oil
4 cloves garlic, minced
1/8 t. red pepper flakes
1 lb. asparagus, cut into
    2-inch pieces
4 tomatoes, chopped
1 c. chicken broth

1/3 c. fresh basil, chopped
salt and pepper to taste
8-oz. pkg. penne, cooked
Garnish: grated Parmesan
    cheese, chopped fresh
    parsley

Heat oil in a large skillet; sauté garlic and red pepper flakes for
2 minutes. Stir in asparagus, tomatoes, broth and basil; cover and
heat for about 8 minutes. Add salt and pepper to taste. Spoon over
cooked penne; sprinkle with Parmesan cheese and parsley.

Host a progressive dinner with several friends. Each family serves one course at their house, as everyone travels from home to home. Start at one place for appetizers, move to the next for soups and salads, again for the main dish and end with dessert!

Kraut & Shells

Makes 4 servings

14-oz. can sauerkraut,
　　drained and rinsed
2 c. medium shells, cooked
1-1/2 lbs. Kielbasa, thickly
　　sliced

3/4 c. butter, melted
1 T. pepper

Combine all ingredients except pepper in a large saucepan; mix well.
Simmer over medium heat until heated through; stir in pepper.

Find a jumbo-size pasta dish for serving up pasta-filled
casseroles...makes helping yourself so much easier!

Parmesan Noodles

Makes 4 to 6 servings

8-oz. pkg. medium egg noodles, cooked
2 T. butter, softened

1/2 c. grated Parmesan cheese
3 T. green onion, chopped
garlic salt and pepper to taste

Toss warm noodles with butter until melted; stir in remaining ingredients. Serve warm or cold.

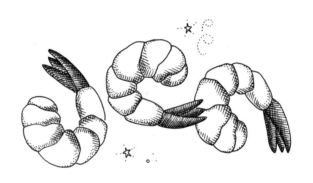

Try flavored pasta...there are so many to choose from!
Pasta flavored with spinach, garlic, basil or even spicy red
peppers adds zest to favorite recipes.

Vermicelli with Shrimp

Makes 4 to 6 servings

1 onion, chopped
2 T. oil
2 cloves garlic, minced
16-oz. can crushed tomatoes
    in purée

1/4 t. red pepper flakes
3/4 t. salt
1 lb. medium shrimp, cleaned
    and cooked
12-oz. pkg. vermicelli, cooked

In a skillet over medium heat, sauté onion in oil until tender, about 5 minutes. Add garlic; cook and stir for 30 seconds. Mix in tomatoes, red pepper flakes and salt; reduce heat and simmer for 10 minutes. Add shrimp; cook over low heat for 4 minutes, stirring occasionally. Stir gently; serve over vermicelli.

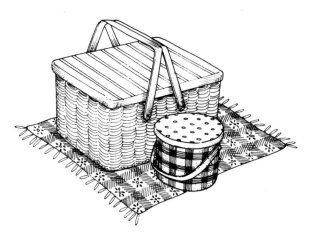

Salad is always tasty with pasta dishes. To keep wooden salad bowls looking their best, rub them inside and out with wax paper after washing them with warm, soapy water. The wax from the paper will keep the surface of the bowl sealed.

Creamy Ham & Noodles

Makes 6 servings

3 c. water
1 T. chicken bouillon granules
8-oz. pkg. wide egg noodles,
   uncooked
1 c. frozen mixed vegetables
1/3 c. onion, chopped

10-3/4 oz. can cream of
   mushroom soup
1/2 c. milk
1/4 t. pepper
1 c. shredded Cheddar cheese
2 c. cooked ham, cubed

In a medium saucepan, bring water and bouillon to a boil over medium-high heat. Stir in uncooked noodles; cover and simmer for 5 minutes, stirring occasionally. Add vegetables and onion. Cover and simmer for an additional 5 minutes, or until noodles are tender and most of liquid is absorbed. Reduce heat to low. Add soup, milk, pepper and Cheddar cheese; mix well. Stir in ham and heat through until cheese is melted.

No man is lonely eating spaghetti, it requires so much attention.
-Christopher Morley

Spaghetti with No-Cook Sauce

Makes 6 servings

2 lbs. tomatoes, diced
1/4 c. sweet onion, diced
2 t. garlic, minced
1/3 c. olive oil

1/4 t. red pepper flakes
16-oz. pkg. spaghetti, cooked
2 c. fresh basil, chopped

Combine tomatoes, onion, garlic, oil and red pepper flakes in a
medium bowl. Cover and let stand at room temperature while
preparing spaghetti. Stir basil into sauce; spoon over hot spaghetti.

Add a few extra cloves of garlic to the pan when cooking pasta.
Combine the extra garlic with 1/2 cup softened butter.
Mix well and chill. Spread on thick slices of Italian bread
and broil for a few minutes until crunchy and golden.

Easy Goulash

Makes 4 to 6 servings

1 lb. ground beef
1/4 c. onion, chopped
14-1/2 oz. can stewed tomatoes
3/4 c. water
2 c. elbow macaroni, uncooked
salt and pepper to taste

15-1/4 oz. can corn, drained
15-oz. can kidney beans,
   drained and rinsed
16-oz. pkg. pasteurized process
   cheese spread, cubed

Brown ground beef and onion in a large saucepan over medium
heat; drain and return to pan. Stir in tomatoes, water, uncooked
macaroni, salt and pepper to taste. Simmer, stirring occasionally, for
8 to 10 minutes, or until macaroni is tender. Add corn, beans and
cheese; continue cooking until heated through and cheese is melted.

Making homemade spaghetti sauce but don't want to stand over a hot pot all day? Place the sauce in an oven-safe dish and bake for an hour at 300 degrees. Pasta-perfect sauce every time!

Cheesy Vegetable Pasta

Makes 3 to 4 servings

2 to 3 cloves garlic, chopped
2 T. butter
2 yellow squash, sliced
2 zucchini, sliced
1/4 c. white wine or vegetable
    broth
1-1/2 to 2 c. milk
8-oz. pkg. pasteurized process
    cheese spread, sliced
pepper to taste
12-oz. pkg. rotini, cooked

In a skillet over medium heat, sauté garlic in butter for 2 minutes.
Add yellow squash and zucchini; sauté for an additional 2 minutes.
Add wine or broth; reduce heat and simmer until tender. Combine
milk, cheese and pepper in a medium saucepan; cook and stir over
medium-low heat until cheese melts. Top rotini with squash and
cheese mixtures; toss to coat.

Making meatballs from scratch? Instead of baking, cook 'em quick by just dropping into boiling water. They'll be lower in fat and will keep their shape too. Boil for a few minutes and they'll be ready to go into sauces or into the freezer for another day.

Seafood Fettuccine

Makes 4 servings

3/4 lb. medium shrimp, cleaned
    and cooked
4-oz. can sliced mushrooms,
    drained
1/2 t. garlic powder
1/8 t. salt
1/8 t. pepper

1/4 c. butter
1/2 c. milk
1/2 c. sour cream
1/2 c. grated Parmesan cheese
8-oz. pkg. fettuccine, cooked
Garnish: chopped fresh parsley

In a skillet over medium heat, sauté shrimp, mushrooms and seasonings in butter for 3 to 5 minutes. Stir in milk, sour cream and Parmesan cheese; gently stir in fettuccine. Warm through over medium heat without boiling. Garnish with parsley.

Make clean-up a snap! Before dinner even starts, fill the sink with hot, soapy water. Put dishes right in when cooking is finished and, by the time dinner and dessert are eaten, cleaning will be a breeze!

54

Garlic-Angel Hair Pasta

Makes 8 servings

7 cloves garlic, minced
1/3 c. olive oil

16-oz. pkg. angel hair, cooked
1-1/3 c. seasoned bread crumbs

In a skillet over low heat, sauté garlic in oil until golden. Pour garlic and oil over cooked pasta; sprinkle with bread crumbs. Mix well; cover and let stand for a few minutes before serving.

You don't have to spend a lot of time setting the table for casual gatherings. Just wrap colorful napkins around silverware and slip them into a glass at each place setting. It's so charming...and you don't have to remember where the forks, knives and spoons go!

Creamy Tomato Penne Pasta

Makes 4 to 6 servings

2 8-oz. cans tomato sauce
garlic powder and white pepper
    to taste
1/2 pt. half-and-half
1 T. grated Parmesan cheese

16-oz. pkg. penne, cooked
Garnish: grated Parmesan
    cheese, chopped fresh
    parsley

Combine tomato sauce, garlic powder and pepper in a small saucepan; stir in half-and-half and Parmesan cheese. Simmer over low heat until heated through. Place cooked penne in a large serving bowl; top with sauce. Garnish with Parmesan cheese and parsley.

Hollow out a round loaf of pumpernickel bread to serve your
Rigatoni & Roasted Vegetables in...a quick and savory meal.

Rigatoni & Roasted Vegetables

Makes 4 servings

1 lb. assorted vegetables such
    as green peppers, zucchini,
    mushrooms and onions, cut
    into bite-size pieces
salt and pepper to taste
2 t. dried rosemary
2 t. dried thyme
2 T. olive oil
8-oz. pkg. rigatoni, cooked
2 t. balsamic vinegar
3 T. grated Parmesan cheese

Arrange vegetables in a lightly greased 13"x9" baking pan. Sprinkle
with seasonings; drizzle oil over all and toss. Bake at 500 degrees
for 10 minutes, until golden and tender. Drain vegetables and set
aside, reserving pan juices. In a large serving bowl, toss together
rigatoni, vegetables, reserved juices as desired and vinegar. Sprinkle
with Parmesan cheese; toss.

No-mess stuffed shells! Instead of a spoon, use a pastry bag
to fill cooked pasta shells...they'll be ready in no time.

Chicken-Stuffed Shells

Makes 6 to 8 servings

1-1/2 c. chicken-flavored
   stuffing mix, prepared
2 c. cooked chicken, chopped
1/2 c. peas
1/2 c. mayonnaise

18 jumbo shells, cooked
10-3/4 oz. can cream of
   chicken soup
2/3 c. water

Combine stuffing, chicken, peas and mayonnaise in a large bowl; spoon into cooked shells. Arrange shells in a greased 13"x9" baking pan. Mix soup and water; pour over shells. Cover and bake at 350 degrees for 30 minutes.

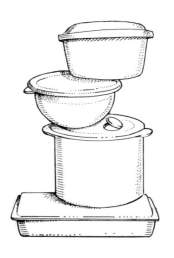

Spray your plastic storage containers with non-stick vegetable spray before pouring tomato-based sauces in...no stains!

Italian Cavatini Bake

Makes 8 to 10 servings

1 lb. ground beef
1 lb. ground Italian pork
    sausage
salt and pepper to taste
28-oz. plus 16-oz. jars
    spaghetti sauce

8-oz. pkg. Italian trio pasta,
    cooked
2 16-oz. pkgs. shredded
    mozzarella cheese
2-1/2 oz. pkg. sliced pepperoni,
    halved

Brown ground beef and sausage in a large skillet over medium heat.
Drain; add salt and pepper to taste. In a lightly greased 13"x9" baking
pan, layer half each of the spaghetti sauce, meat mixture, cooked
pasta, mozzarella cheese and pepperoni; repeat layers. Bake at
350 degrees for 45 minutes.

A pat of homemade garlic butter really adds flavor to warm bread or steamed vegetables. Blend equal parts of softened butter and olive oil, then stir in finely chopped garlic to taste....so easy!

Mom's Lasagna Rolls

Makes 6 servings

1 lb. ground pork sausage,
 browned and drained
8-oz. plus 3-oz. pkgs. cream
 cheese, diced
1 bunch green onions, chopped
1 green pepper, diced

28-oz. jar spaghetti sauce,
 divided
12-oz. pkg. lasagna, uncooked
1-1/2 c. shredded mozzarella
 cheese

Brown sausage in a skillet over medium heat; drain. Add cream
cheese; stir over low heat until melted. Stir in onions and green pepper;
remove from heat. Spread half of spaghetti sauce in a lightly greased
13"x9" baking pan; set aside. Cook lasagna just until tender; remove
from heat but do not drain. Lay lasagna flat, one strip at a time; spoon
one to 2 tablespoons sausage mixture at one end. Slowly roll up
lasagna; place in baking pan seam-side down. Repeat with remaining
lasagna. Top with remaining sauce and mozzarella cheese. Bake at
350 degrees for 15 to 20 minutes, until bubbly and cheese is melted.

Roasted garlic is heavenly to spread on bread and so easy in the microwave! Slice the top off a whole garlic bulb and set it in a microwave-safe container. Sprinkle to taste with salt, pepper and olive oil, add a little water and cover with plastic wrap. Heat on high setting for 8 minutes, or until soft.

Baked Turkey-Spinach Penne

Makes 12 servings

1 lb. ground turkey
1 onion, chopped
3 cloves garlic, chopped
1/3 t. cayenne pepper
28-oz. can diced tomatoes
1/3 c. pesto sauce

16-oz. pkg. penne, cooked
10-oz. pkg. spinach, torn
8-oz. pkg. mozzarella cheese,
    cubed
1 c. grated Parmesan cheese,
    divided

Brown turkey, onion, garlic and cayenne pepper in a large saucepan over medium heat; drain. Add tomatoes and simmer until thickened, stirring occasionally. Remove from heat; stir in pesto and set aside. In a large bowl, combine cooked penne, spinach, mozzarella cheese and 1/3 cup Parmesan; stir in turkey mixture. Spoon into a lightly greased 13"x9" baking pan; sprinkle with remaining cheese. Bake at 375 degrees for 30 minutes.

Vintage-style souvenir tea towels make whimsical oversized napkins...handy for messy-but-tasty foods!

Family Night Noodle Bake

Makes 8 servings

1 lb. ground beef
1/2 lb. ground pork
2 T. butter
2/3 c. onion, chopped
2 10-3/4 oz. cans tomato soup
3-oz. pkg. cream cheese, cubed
2 T. sugar

2 t. Worcestershire sauce
1 t. salt
1/4 t. pepper
2 c. wide egg noodles, cooked
1 c. corn flake cereal, crushed
1/2 c. butter, melted

In a large skillet over medium heat, brown beef and pork in butter.
Add onion and cook until tender but not browned; drain. Stir in soup,
cream cheese, sugar, Worcestershire sauce, salt and pepper. Reduce
heat and simmer for 15 minutes. Place cooked noodles in a greased
11"x7" baking pan; pour meat mixture over noodles. Toss together
cereal and melted butter; sprinkle over top. Bake at 350 degrees for
20 minutes, or until heated through.

Make cheese curls quickly for garnishing salads...simply pull
a vegetable peeler across a block of cheese.

One-Dish Macaroni & Cheese *Makes 8 to 10 servings*

14-oz. pkg. elbow macaroni,
    uncooked
2 10-3/4 oz. cans Cheddar
    cheese soup

3-1/2 c. milk
16-oz. pkg. shredded
    Cheddar cheese

Combine uncooked macaroni with remaining ingredients in a greased
3-quart casserole dish. Cover and bake at 350 degrees for one hour.
Uncover and bake an additional 20 minutes.

Pick up a dozen pint Mason jars...perfect for serving
cold beverages at informal gatherings.

Pizza Pasta Casserole

Makes 12 servings

2 lbs. ground beef
1 onion, chopped
2 28-oz. jars spaghetti sauce
16-oz. pkg. rotini, cooked

16-oz. pkg. shredded
   mozzarella cheese, divided
8-oz. pkg. sliced pepperoni,
   divided

Brown ground beef with onion in a large skillet over medium heat; drain. Stir in spaghetti sauce and cooked rotini; spread equally in two greased 13"x9" baking pans. Sprinkle both with mozzarella cheese; arrange pepperoni slices on top. Bake at 350 degrees for 25 to 30 minutes.

Take the kids to a paint-your-own pottery shop! Let them decorate cheery plates and bowls for the whole family. Their creations will warm hearts and tummies at the same time.

Bake & Take Chicken Vermicelli

Makes 8 servings

1 c. chicken broth
16-oz. pkg. vermicelli,
    uncooked
10-3/4 oz. can cream of
    mushroom soup
4 c. cooked chicken, cubed
1 onion, diced

1/2 c. green pepper, chopped
2-oz. jar chopped pimentos,
    drained
1 t. salt
1 t. pepper
16-oz. container shredded sharp
    Cheddar cheese, divided

Bring broth to a boil over medium heat in a large saucepan.
Break vermicelli coarsely; cook just until tender. Drain; place in a
lightly greased 13"x9" baking pan. Mix in soup, chicken, onion,
green pepper, pimentos, salt, pepper and half the cheese; cover and
refrigerate overnight. Sprinkle with remaining cheese. Bake at
350 degrees for 45 minutes.

Slip sparkly bangle bracelets around
rolled dinner napkins for playful table settings!

Spinach-Noodle Bake

Makes 10 to 12 servings

3 eggs, beaten
8-oz. container cottage cheese
8-oz. container sour cream
16-oz. pkg. spinach egg
  noodles, cooked

2 10-oz. pkgs. frozen chopped
  spinach, thawed and
  drained
salt and pepper to taste
3/4 c. shredded Cheddar cheese

Blend eggs, cottage cheese and sour cream in a small bowl; set aside.
Combine cooked noodles and spinach in a large bowl; add egg
mixture, salt and pepper to taste. Spread in a greased 13"x9" baking
pan; top with Cheddar cheese. Bake at 350 degrees for 40 minutes.

Pour olive oil into saucers and sprinkle with a little Italian seasoning...perfect for dipping slices of warm crusty bread.

Reuben Casserole

Makes 6 servings

8-oz. pkg. wide egg noodles, cooked
1/4 c. butter, softened and divided
14-1/2 oz. can sauerkraut, drained and rinsed
12-oz. can corned beef, diced

8-oz. pkg. shredded Swiss cheese
1 tomato, sliced
1/2 c. Thousand Island salad dressing
1/2 c. fresh rye bread crumbs
1/2 t. caraway seed

Toss cooked noodles in a large bowl with 2 tablespoons butter, sauerkraut and corned beef. Add Swiss cheese and lightly toss; spread in a greased 13"x9" baking pan. Layer tomato slices on top; cover with salad dressing and set aside. Melt remaining butter in a small skillet over medium heat. Cook bread crumbs and caraway until golden; sprinkle over top. Bake at 350 degrees for one hour.

Everything you see I owe to spaghetti.

-Sophia Loren

Baked Spaghetti Ring

Makes 4 to 6 servings

16-oz. pkg. spaghetti, cooked
2 10-oz. pkgs. frozen chopped
    spinach, cooked and drained
1/4 c. onion, chopped

4 eggs, beaten
1-1/3 c. grated Parmesan cheese
Optional: spaghetti sauce,
    warmed

Mix all ingredients except spaghetti sauce together; pour into a
greased Bundt® pan. Cover and bake at 375 degrees for 25 to
30 minutes. Let stand 5 minutes; turn out of pan onto a serving
platter. If desired, garnish with a small bowl of warmed spaghetti
sauce set in center of ring.

March a collection of herb plants in tiny pots across the kitchen windowsill...oh-so sweet and handy for last-minute seasoning.

Ravioli Casserole

Makes 6 to 8 servings

28-oz. jar spaghetti sauce,
   divided
25-oz. pkg. frozen cheese
   ravioli, cooked and divided
16-oz. container cottage cheese,
   divided

16-oz. pkg. shredded
   mozzarella cheese, divided
1/4 c. grated Parmesan cheese

Spread 1/2 cup spaghetti sauce in a lightly greased 13"x9" baking
pan; layer with half the ravioli. Pour 1-1/4 cups sauce over ravioli.
Spread one cup cottage cheese over top; sprinkle with 2 cups
mozzarella cheese. Repeat layers; sprinkle with Parmesan cheese.
Bake, uncovered, at 350 degrees for 30 to 40 minutes. Let stand
5 to 10 minutes before serving.

Having a picnic on a breezy day? Cast-off clip earrings make sparkly tablecloth weights...simply clip 'em to the 4 corners of the cloth.

Chicken & Mushroom Bake

Makes 6 servings

6 boneless, skinless chicken breasts, cooked and cubed
16-oz. pkg. medium egg noodles, cooked
8-oz. can sliced water chestnuts, drained
2 10-3/4 oz. cans cream of mushroom soup
1-1/2 c. chicken broth
1 c. milk
1 onion, chopped
12-oz. pkg. shredded Cheddar cheese
2-oz. jar chopped pimentos, drained
1 t. salt
pepper to taste

Combine all ingredients in a large bowl. Spread in a greased 13"x9" baking pan; cover and refrigerate overnight. Bake at 325 degrees for 60 to 70 minutes. Let stand for 15 minutes; cut into squares.

A tin school lunchbox is perfect for storing favorite recipes.

Down-Home Tuna Casserole

Makes 4 servings

8-oz. pkg. medium egg
　　noodles, cooked
2 T. butter
1 c. celery, chopped
1/4 c. onion, chopped
10-3/4 oz. can cream of
　　mushroom soup
3/4 c. milk

2 T. all-purpose flour
1/4 t. dried thyme
1/4 t. pepper
9-1/4 oz. can tuna, drained
1 sleeve round buttery crackers,
　　crushed
1/4 c. grated Parmesan cheese

Place cooked noodles in a greased 1-1/2 quart casserole dish; set
aside. Melt butter in a small saucepan over medium heat. Sauté celery
and onion until tender; stir into noodles. Blend soup, milk, flour and
seasonings in a small bowl; blend well and add tuna. Combine with
noodles; mix well. Toss together crushed crackers and Parmesan
cheese; sprinkle over top. Bake at 350 degrees for 25 minutes.

Use new plastic sand pails to serve ice at parties...use a
sand shovel as a server!

Spaghetti Pie

Makes 6 servings

8-oz. pkg. spaghetti, cooked
2 eggs, beaten
1/4 c. grated Parmesan cheese
1/2 t. salt
3-1/2 oz. pkg. sliced pepperoni,
    divided

8-oz. pkg. shredded mozzarella
    cheese, divided
2 c. spaghetti sauce, warmed

Combine cooked spaghetti, eggs, Parmesan cheese and salt in a
large bowl; mix well. Spread half of spaghetti mixture in a greased
13"x9" baking pan. Layer with half each of pepperoni slices and
mozzarella cheese; spread remaining spaghetti mixture over top.
Bake at 350 degrees for 15 to 20 minutes, until hot and bubbly.
Cut into squares; serve topped with warmed sauce.

Get mouths watering in anticipation with a
big ceramic bowl just for pasta.

Ranchero Macaroni Bake

Makes 8 servings

26-oz. can cream of
    mushroom soup
1 c. milk
12-oz. pkg. shredded Cheddar
    cheese

1 c. salsa
6 c. elbow macaroni, cooked
1 c. tortilla chips, coarsely
    crushed

Combine soup and milk in a large bowl. Stir in Cheddar cheese, salsa and cooked macaroni. Spoon into a lightly greased 3-quart casserole dish. Bake at 400 degrees for 20 minutes. Stir; sprinkle with crushed chips. Bake for an additional 5 minutes, or until hot and bubbly.

Scour tag sales for big, old-fashioned enamelware stockpots.
they're just the right size for family-size portions of pasta dishes.

Lip-Smackin' Stuffed Shells   *Makes 10 to 12 servings*

16-oz. pkg. shredded
  mozzarella cheese
16-oz. container cottage cheese
15-oz. can tomato sauce
2 eggs, beaten
2 10-oz. pkgs. frozen chopped
  spinach, thawed and
  drained

1/8 t. nutmeg
salt and pepper to taste
28-oz. jar spaghetti sauce,
  divided
12-oz. pkg. jumbo shells,
  cooked
Garnish: grated Parmesan
  cheese

Combine cheeses, tomato sauce, eggs, spinach and seasonings in a
large bowl; mix well and set aside. Spread 1/4 cup spaghetti sauce
evenly in a lightly greased 13"x9" baking pan. Spoon cheese mixture
evenly into shells; arrange stuffed-side up over sauce. Pour remaining
sauce over shells; sprinkle with Parmesan cheese. Bake at 350 degrees
for 30 minutes.

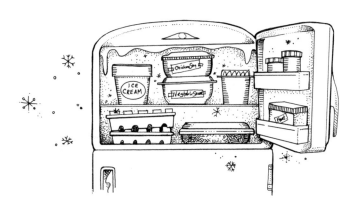

To freeze a just-made casserole, let it stand at room
temperature for 30 minutes, then refrigerate for 30 minutes
more. When cool, wrap it tightly with heavy-duty aluminum
foil...label and freeze up to 3 months.

Johnny Marzetti

Makes 4 to 6 servings

1 lb. ground beef
1 onion, chopped
1 green pepper, chopped
28-oz. jar spaghetti sauce

1-1/2 c. elbow macaroni, cooked
8-oz. pkg. shredded Cheddar cheese

In a skillet over medium heat, cook ground beef, onion and green pepper until beef is browned and vegetables are tender. Drain; stir in spaghetti sauce and macaroni. Pour into a lightly greased 13"x9" baking pan; sprinkle with Cheddar cheese. Bake at 350 degrees for 30 minutes, or until hot and bubbly.

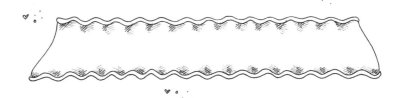

Make this casserole the night before and
store in the fridge for an even speedier dinner.
Just add 10 minutes to the baking time...so easy!

Broccoli-Chicken Lasagna

Makes 4 to 6 servings

1/4 c. butter
1/4 c. all-purpose flour
1 T. chicken bouillon granules
pepper to taste
1/2 t. Italian seasoning
2 c. milk

8-oz. pkg. shredded
   Italian-blend cheese
1 c. cooked chicken, diced
2 c. broccoli flowerets, cooked
4 strips lasagna, cooked

Melt butter in a saucepan over medium-low heat; stir in flour, bouillon, pepper and Italian seasoning. Gradually stir in milk; cook and stir until thickened. Add Italian-blend cheese; stir until melted. Mix in chicken and broccoli. Spread 1/2 cup mixture in the bottom of an 8"x8" baking pan sprayed with non-stick vegetable spray. Top with half the lasagna and half the remaining sauce; repeat layers. Bake, uncovered, at 350 degrees for 30 to 40 minutes. Let stand for several minutes before cutting into squares.

Turn any casserole into an overnight time-saver. Simply prepare
a favorite casserole recipe the night before, cover and
refrigerate. Just add 15 to 20 minutes to the baking time!

Pasta di Carla

Makes 6 to 8 servings

1 lb. ground Italian pork
  sausage
1 green pepper, chopped
1 red pepper, chopped
1 onion, chopped
2 14-1/2 oz. cans Italian-style
  diced tomatoes

8-oz. pkg. sliced mushrooms
16-oz. pkg. rigatoni, cooked
28-oz. jar spaghetti sauce
12-oz. pkg. shredded
  mozzarella cheese, divided
Italian seasoning to taste

Brown sausage in a large skillet over medium heat. Add peppers and onions and sauté until tender; drain. Add tomatoes and mushrooms; simmer until heated through. Combine sausage mixture with cooked rigatoni and spaghetti sauce; mix well to coat rigatoni. Add 2-1/2 cups mozzarella; sprinkle with Italian seasoning to taste. Stir to blend; pour into a lightly greased 13"x9" baking pan. Bake at 350 degrees for 20 to 25 minutes, until heated through and cheese is melted. Serve in bowls, sprinkled with remaining mozzarella.

Baking soda can bring out the natural sweetness of tomato sauce by reducing the acid. Add about 1/4 teaspoon per quart of sauce as it simmers.

Quick & Easy Lasagna

Makes 12 servings

1 lb. ground beef
3 15-oz. cans tomato sauce
16-oz. pkg. lasagna, cooked

16-oz. container cottage cheese
16-oz. pkg. shredded
   mozzarella cheese

Brown ground beef in a skillet; drain. Stir in sauce; spread 1/4 cup of sauce mixture in a lightly greased 13"x9" baking pan. Arrange half the cooked lasagna in the pan. Pour half the remaining sauce mixture over lasagna; spoon on half the cottage cheese. Sprinkle with half the mozzarella cheese. Repeat layers, ending with mozzarella. Bake at 350 degrees until cheese melts, about 20 to 25 minutes. Let stand for a few minutes; cut into squares.

The trouble with eating Italian food is that
5 or 6 days later you're hungry again.
-George Miller

Creamy Salmon Manicotti

Makes 4 to 6 servings

7.1-oz. pkg. boneless, skinless
    pink salmon, flaked
16-oz. container ricotta cheese
1 egg, beaten

8 manicotti shells, cooked
16-oz. jar Alfredo sauce
Garnish: dill weed

In a medium bowl, combine salmon, ricotta cheese and egg until well mixed. Using a small spoon, fill each manicotti shell; if there is any filling left, stir into Alfredo sauce. Arrange filled manicotti in a lightly greased 11"x7" baking pan. Pour sauce over manicotti; sprinkle with dill weed. Bake, covered, at 350 degrees for 35 to 40 minutes.

Mix & match different colors and patterns
of place settings, just for fun!

Spaghetti Deluxe

Makes 4 servings

1 onion, chopped
1 T. oil
1 lb. ground beef
1 t. salt
1/8 t. pepper

3 c. cooked spaghetti, divided
14-1/2 oz. can diced tomatoes
12-oz. pkg. shredded Cheddar
   cheese

Sauté onion in oil in a skillet over medium heat. Add ground beef and cook until browned. Drain; stir in salt and pepper and set aside. Layer one cup spaghetti in a lightly greased 13"x9" baking pan; top with beef mixture. Layer with remaining spaghetti and tomatoes; sprinkle with cheese. Cover and bake at 350 degrees for 35 minutes; uncover and bake for an additional 10 minutes.

Potted placecards...pick up some herb seedlings,
plant them in tiny terra cotta pots and add popsicle-stick markers
with each guest's name. Choose herbs that pair perfectly with
pasta dishes such as oregano, basil and parsley.

Ring Toss Salad

Makes 4 to 6 servings

7-oz. pkg. wagon wheels,
    cooked
1 head cabbage, shredded
1 cucumber, chopped
1/2 green pepper, chopped
1/4 c. green onion, sliced
1 c. mayonnaise
1/2 c. sugar
1-1/2 t. vinegar

Place wagon wheels in a large bowl; toss with vegetables and set aside. Combine mayonnaise, sugar and vinegar in a small bowl; stir into pasta mixture to coat. Chill.

Yankee Doodle went to town,
A-riding on a pony,
He stuck a feather in his hat,
And called it macaroni.

-Early American song

Grandma's Macaroni Salad   *Makes 6 to 8 servings*

8-oz. pkg. elbow macaroni,
   cooked
1 egg, hard-boiled, peeled
   and chopped
1 carrot, peeled and grated
1 tomato, chopped
1 onion, chopped
2 stalks celery, chopped

1 green pepper, chopped
1 t. salt
pepper to taste
fresh parsley to taste, chopped
5 T. mayonnaise
3 T. vinegar
3 T. olive oil
Garnish: paprika

In a large bowl, combine macaroni with egg, vegetables, salt, pepper and parsley; set aside. Mix together remaining ingredients except paprika in a small bowl; toss with macaroni mixture. Sprinkle with paprika; chill.

Making salad croutons at home is easy! Cube 4 slices of bread and place in a shallow baking pan. Combine 3 tablespoons melted butter with 1/4 teaspoon garlic powder and toss with bread. Bake for 30 minutes in a 300-degree oven, until crisp.

BLT Salad

8-oz. pkg. elbow macaroni,
    cooked
4 c. tomatoes, chopped
4 slices bacon, crisply cooked
    and crumbled
1/2 c. mayonnaise
1/3 c. sour cream

1 T. Dijon mustard
2 t. cider vinegar
1 t. sugar
1/2 t. salt
1/2 t. pepper
3 c. lettuce, shredded

Place macaroni in a large bowl. Add tomatoes and bacon; toss gently
and set aside. Mix remaining ingredients except lettuce together in a
small bowl; stir well. Pour over macaroni mixture; gently toss until
well coated. Chill; serve over shredded lettuce.

Hollowed-out peppers become fun salad bowls! They're just
the right size and add a splash of color to the table.

Antipasto Tortellini Salad

Makes 8 servings

16-oz. pkg. cheese tortellini, cooked
1/4 lb. deli salami, cubed
1/4 lb. deli provolone cheese, cut into strips
6-oz. jar marinated artichokes, drained and sliced

6-oz. can sliced black olives, drained and divided
1-1/2 c. Italian salad dressing
1/2 c. grated Parmesan cheese

In a large bowl, combine tortellini, salami, provolone, artichokes and 1/2 cup olives; set aside. Combine dressing and Parmesan; pour over tortellini mixture and toss gently. Top with remaining olives. Chill for one to 2 hours.

Sharing a pasta dish or salad? Be sure to tie on a tag with the recipe. Clever tags can be made from almost anything...mailing or gift tags, decorated notecards, ribbons and colorful labels.

Tuna Seashell Salad

Makes 6 to 8 servings

16-oz. pkg. small shell
    macaroni, cooked
12-oz. can tuna, drained
1/2 to 1 c. mayonnaise-type
    salad dressing
1/4 c. sweet pickle relish

3 eggs, hard-boiled, peeled
    and diced
1/4 lb. mild Cheddar cheese,
    diced

Combine all ingredients in a large bowl; chill.

For a little extra zing, add a squeeze of
lemon or lime to any salad!

Greek Perfection Pasta Salad *Makes 8 to 10 servings*

16-oz. pkg. rainbow rotini,
  cooked
6-oz. pkg. pepperoni, sliced
5-3/4 oz. jar sliced green olives,
  drained
2-1/4 oz. can sliced black
  olives, drained

8-oz. pkg. crumbled feta cheese
1 tomato, diced
Optional: 1/4 c. onion, diced
fresh parsley and basil to taste,
  chopped
16-oz. bottle Italian salad
  dressing

Combine all ingredients except salad dressing in a large bowl. Pour
dressing to taste over top; toss to coat. Chill at least one to 2 hours
before serving.

Taking a pasta salad to a picnic? Mix it up in a plastic zipping bag instead of a bowl, seal and set it right on the counter. No worries about spills or leaks!

Cucumber & Tomato Salad

Makes 10 to 12 servings

16-oz. pkg. thin spaghetti,
    cooked
1 cucumber, peeled and diced
1 tomato, diced

1 sweet onion, diced
1/4 c. salad seasoning
8-oz. bottle Italian salad
    dressing

Arrange spaghetti in a large bowl. Add vegetables and seasoning;
mix gently. Stir in desired amount salad dressing. Chill.

Shake up a recipe for a change of pace. Use fettuccine or angel hair pasta in main dishes or try rotini or wagon wheel pasta in salads.

Chicken & Spirals Salad

Makes 8 servings

8-oz. pkg. rainbow rotini, cooked
4 boneless, skinless chicken breasts, cooked and diced
11-oz. can mandarin oranges, drained
1 sweet onion, chopped
1 green pepper, chopped
3 stalks celery, chopped
8-oz. can water chestnuts, drained and chopped
1/2 lb. seedless green grapes, halved
1-1/2 to 2 c. ranch salad dressing

Place rotini in a large bowl. Add remaining ingredients in order listed. Toss together and chill.

Vintage swanky swig glasses make the prettiest
tealight holders to dress up the dinner table.
Their colorful, retro designs really shine through!

Shrimp & Seashell Salad

Makes 4 to 6 servings

2 c. small shell macaroni,
    cooked
1 c. tiny shrimp, cooked
    and peeled
2 T. onion, chopped
3 stalks celery, chopped
1-1/2 c. carrots, peeled and
    grated

2 c. frozen peas
3/4 c. mayonnaise-style
    salad dressing
1/2 c. French salad dressing
1 t. salt
1/4 t. garlic powder
Garnish: shoestring potatoes

Combine macaroni, shrimp and vegetables in a large bowl; toss well and set aside. Combine salad dressings, salt and garlic powder in a small bowl; blend well and toss with macaroni mixture. Chill; garnish with shoestring potatoes.

Combine ingredients for homemade salad dressing in a squeeze bottle instead of a bowl. Shake bottle to incorporate flavors and squeeze onto salad...what could be easier?

Springtime Pasta Salad

Makes 8 servings

16-oz. pkg. rotini, cooked
2 t. oil
1-1/2 c. vinegar
1-1/2 c. sugar
1 T. dried parsley
2 t. mustard
1 t. garlic salt

1 t. salt
1 t. pepper
1 onion, chopped
1 cucumber, peeled and chopped
2-oz. jar chopped pimentos,
    drained

Toss rotini with oil in a large bowl. Add remaining ingredients; mix well. Chill for 2 to 3 days before serving, stirring occasionally.

INDEX

INDEX

How Did Gooseberry Patch Get Started?

Gooseberry Patch started in 1984 one day over the backyard fence in Delaware, Ohio. We were next-door neighbors who shared a love of collecting antiques, gardening and country decorating. Though neither of us had any experience (Jo Ann was a first-grade school teacher and Vickie, a flight attendant & legal secretary), we decided to try our hands at the mail-order business. Since we both had young children, this was perfect for us. We could work from our kitchen tables and keep an eye on the kids too! As our children grew, so did our "little" business. We moved into our own building in the country and filled the shelves to the brim with kitchenware, candles, gourmet goodies, enamelware, bowls and our very own line of cookbooks, calendars and organizers. We're so glad you're a part of our **Gooseberry Patch** family!

For a free copy of our **Gooseberry Patch**
catalog, write us, call us or visit us online at:

Gooseberry Patch
600 London Rd.
★ P.O. Box 190 ★
Delaware, OH 43015

1·800·854·6673
www.gooseberrypatch.com